ATLAS

OF

KALAMAZOO CO.

MICHIGAN.

From Recent Actual Surveys and Records

Under the Superintendence of

F. W. BEERS,

PUBLISHED BY

F. W. BEERS & CO.

36 Vesey St.

NEW YORK.

1873.

TABLE OF CONTENTS.

EXPLANATIONS FOR THIS ATLAS.

Rail Roads in operation	DETROIT AND BAY CITY R.R.
Proposed Rail Roads	PROPOSED R. R.
Public Roads	
Rivers	FLINT RIVER
Farm Lines	
Section Lines	
Quarter Section Lines	
Township Lines	
School District Lines	
Style of Figures used to denote section numbers	35
Style of Figures used to denote areas of farms	176⁹
Distances on roads from one Branch or Cross Road to another	161

PRACTICAL DESCRIPTION OF SECTIONAL LANDS.

North-west quarter of Section 10, in Township 18, North of Range 7, East of the Third Principal Meridian. 160 A.

TABLE OF DISTANCES
FOR
Kalamazoo County, Mich.

THESE DISTANCES ARE GIVEN IN MILES AND TENTHS, BY ACTUAL MEASUREMENT BETWEEN VILLAGES, ON THE NEAREST PUBLIC ROADS.

	Alamo	Augusta	Climax	Comstock	Cooper	Fulton	Galesburgh	KALAMAZOO	Oshtemo	Pavilion	Portage	Richland	Schoolcraft	South Climax	Scott	Vicksburg	Wakeshma	Yorkville
Alamo	0.																	
Augusta	18.2	0.																
Climax	21.	7.	0.															
Comstock	11.5	8.8	9.5	0.														
Cooper	5.	13.4	16.8	7.8	0.													
Fulton	25.2	16.5	8.5	14.4	22.	0.												
Galesburgh	15.3	4.6	5.3	5.	11.5	12.5	0.											
KALAMAZOO	8.5	12.2	13.	3.5	6.	19.8	8.5	0.										
Oshtemo	8.	17.5	17.5	8.9	8.7	19.3	13.7	5.4	0.									
Pavilion	19.6	12.2	6.7	9.	16.6	5.5	8.	11.1	13.9	0.								
Portage	13.2	15.4	13.1	7.2	12.	13.5	10.9	6.1	6.	8.4	0.							
Richland	12.7	5.8	11.2	6.5	7.8	18.6	6.2	5.7	14.	14.	13.8	0.						
Schoolcraft	17.9	20.9	17.2	13.2	17.6	14.2	16.3	12.	10.	10.9	6.	19.6	0.					
South Climax	22.7	11.4	4.5	11.4	19.	4.	8.5	14.2	17.7	4.2	12.4	14.8	15.	0.				
Scott	19.2	10.4	5.	8.	15.6	6.4	6.5	10.6	14.	1.8	8.9	12.5	12.3	3.6	0.			
Vicksburg	20.	17.8	13.	12.	18.3	9.	13.4	12.4	12.5	6.3	6.7	13.2	5.4	10.	8.	0.		
Wakeshma	26.1	14.2	7.2	14.9	22.6	3.	12.	17.6	20.8	7.	15.2	18.1	16.8	3.5	6.9	11.5	0.	
Yorkville	16.4	3.6	10.	8.	10.5	18.	5.8	10.8	16.2	14.	15.2	3.2	5.21	14.	12.8	19.	17.1	0.

STATISTICS OF KALAMAZOO COUNTY, MICHIGAN, COLLECTED BY THE U. S., FOR THE NINTH CENSUS, COMPILED IN THE STATE DEPARTMENT OF MICHIGAN.

Agricultural Productions of KALAMAZOO CO., by Townships.	Acres of Land: Improved.	Unimproved: Wood Land.	Unimproved: Other Land Unimproved.	Present Cash Value: Of Farms.	Present Cash Value: Of Farming Implements.	Total amount of wages paid, including board.	Horses.	Mules and Asses.	Milch Cows.	Working Oxen.	Other Cattle.	Sheep.	Swine.	Value of all Live Stock.	Wheat: Spring.	Wheat: Winter.	Indian Corn.	Oats.	Barley.	Buckwheat.	Wool.	Potatoes.	Orchard Products.	Butter.	Cheese.	Hay.	Clover Seed.	Hops.	Forest Products.	Value of Animals Slaughtered, or sold for Slaughter.	Estimated value of all farm productions, including betterments and additions to stock.
	2 No.	3 No.	4 No.	5 D.	6 D.	7 D.	8 No.	9 No.	10 No.	11 No.	12 No.	13 No.	14 No.	15 D.	16 B.	17 B.	19 B.	20 B.	21 B.	22 B.	23 P.	24 B.	30 D.	33 P.	34 P.	36 T.	37 B.	39 P.	40 D.	41 D.	42 D.
KALAMAZOO CO.	[illegible]	[illegible]	[illegible]	[illegible]	[illegible]	[illegible]	[illegible]	[illegible]	[illegible]	[illegible]	[illegible]	[illegible]	[illegible]	[illegible]	[illegible]	[illegible]	[illegible]	[illegible]	[illegible]	[illegible]	[illegible]	[illegible]	[illegible]	[illegible]	[illegible]	[illegible]	[illegible]	[illegible]	[illegible]	[illegible]	[illegible]
Alamo	[illegible]	[illegible]	[illegible]	[illegible]	[illegible]	[illegible]	[illegible]	[illegible]	[illegible]	[illegible]	[illegible]	[illegible]	[illegible]	[illegible]	[illegible]	[illegible]	[illegible]	[illegible]	[illegible]	[illegible]	[illegible]	[illegible]	[illegible]	[illegible]	[illegible]	[illegible]	[illegible]	[illegible]	[illegible]	[illegible]	[illegible]
Brady	[illegible]	[illegible]	[illegible]	[illegible]	[illegible]	[illegible]	[illegible]	[illegible]	[illegible]	[illegible]	[illegible]	[illegible]	[illegible]	[illegible]	[illegible]	[illegible]	[illegible]	[illegible]	[illegible]	[illegible]	[illegible]	[illegible]	[illegible]	[illegible]	[illegible]	[illegible]	[illegible]	[illegible]	[illegible]	[illegible]	[illegible]
Charleston	[illegible]	[illegible]	[illegible]	[illegible]	[illegible]	[illegible]	[illegible]	[illegible]	[illegible]	[illegible]	[illegible]	[illegible]	[illegible]	[illegible]	[illegible]	[illegible]	[illegible]	[illegible]	[illegible]	[illegible]	[illegible]	[illegible]	[illegible]	[illegible]	[illegible]	[illegible]	[illegible]	[illegible]	[illegible]	[illegible]	[illegible]
Climax	[illegible]	[illegible]	[illegible]	[illegible]	[illegible]	[illegible]	[illegible]	[illegible]	[illegible]	[illegible]	[illegible]	[illegible]	[illegible]	[illegible]	[illegible]	[illegible]	[illegible]	[illegible]	[illegible]	[illegible]	[illegible]	[illegible]	[illegible]	[illegible]	[illegible]	[illegible]	[illegible]	[illegible]	[illegible]	[illegible]	[illegible]
Comstock	[illegible]	[illegible]	[illegible]	[illegible]	[illegible]	[illegible]	[illegible]	[illegible]	[illegible]	[illegible]	[illegible]	[illegible]	[illegible]	[illegible]	[illegible]	[illegible]	[illegible]	[illegible]	[illegible]	[illegible]	[illegible]	[illegible]	[illegible]	[illegible]	[illegible]	[illegible]	[illegible]	[illegible]	[illegible]	[illegible]	[illegible]
Cooper	[illegible]	[illegible]	[illegible]	[illegible]	[illegible]	[illegible]	[illegible]	[illegible]	[illegible]	[illegible]	[illegible]	[illegible]	[illegible]	[illegible]	[illegible]	[illegible]	[illegible]	[illegible]	[illegible]	[illegible]	[illegible]	[illegible]	[illegible]	[illegible]	[illegible]	[illegible]	[illegible]	[illegible]	[illegible]	[illegible]	[illegible]
Kalamazoo	[illegible]	[illegible]	[illegible]	[illegible]	[illegible]	[illegible]	[illegible]	[illegible]	[illegible]	[illegible]	[illegible]	[illegible]	[illegible]	[illegible]	[illegible]	[illegible]	[illegible]	[illegible]	[illegible]	[illegible]	[illegible]	[illegible]	[illegible]	[illegible]	[illegible]	[illegible]	[illegible]	[illegible]	[illegible]	[illegible]	[illegible]
Oshtemo	[illegible]	[illegible]	[illegible]	[illegible]	[illegible]	[illegible]	[illegible]	[illegible]	[illegible]	[illegible]	[illegible]	[illegible]	[illegible]	[illegible]	[illegible]	[illegible]	[illegible]	[illegible]	[illegible]	[illegible]	[illegible]	[illegible]	[illegible]	[illegible]	[illegible]	[illegible]	[illegible]	[illegible]	[illegible]	[illegible]	[illegible]
Pavilion	[illegible]	[illegible]	[illegible]	[illegible]	[illegible]	[illegible]	[illegible]	[illegible]	[illegible]	[illegible]	[illegible]	[illegible]	[illegible]	[illegible]	[illegible]	[illegible]	[illegible]	[illegible]	[illegible]	[illegible]	[illegible]	[illegible]	[illegible]	[illegible]	[illegible]	[illegible]	[illegible]	[illegible]	[illegible]	[illegible]	[illegible]
Portage	[illegible]	[illegible]	[illegible]	[illegible]	[illegible]	[illegible]	[illegible]	[illegible]	[illegible]	[illegible]	[illegible]	[illegible]	[illegible]	[illegible]	[illegible]	[illegible]	[illegible]	[illegible]	[illegible]	[illegible]	[illegible]	[illegible]	[illegible]	[illegible]	[illegible]	[illegible]	[illegible]	[illegible]	[illegible]	[illegible]	[illegible]
Prairie Ronde	[illegible]	[illegible]	[illegible]	[illegible]	[illegible]	[illegible]	[illegible]	[illegible]	[illegible]	[illegible]	[illegible]	[illegible]	[illegible]	[illegible]	[illegible]	[illegible]	[illegible]	[illegible]	[illegible]	[illegible]	[illegible]	[illegible]	[illegible]	[illegible]	[illegible]	[illegible]	[illegible]	[illegible]	[illegible]	[illegible]	[illegible]
Richland	[illegible]	[illegible]	[illegible]	[illegible]	[illegible]	[illegible]	[illegible]	[illegible]	[illegible]	[illegible]	[illegible]	[illegible]	[illegible]	[illegible]	[illegible]	[illegible]	[illegible]	[illegible]	[illegible]	[illegible]	[illegible]	[illegible]	[illegible]	[illegible]	[illegible]	[illegible]	[illegible]	[illegible]	[illegible]	[illegible]	[illegible]
Ross	[illegible]	[illegible]	[illegible]	[illegible]	[illegible]	[illegible]	[illegible]	[illegible]	[illegible]	[illegible]	[illegible]	[illegible]	[illegible]	[illegible]	[illegible]	[illegible]	[illegible]	[illegible]	[illegible]	[illegible]	[illegible]	[illegible]	[illegible]	[illegible]	[illegible]	[illegible]	[illegible]	[illegible]	[illegible]	[illegible]	[illegible]
Schoolcraft	[illegible]	[illegible]	[illegible]	[illegible]	[illegible]	[illegible]	[illegible]	[illegible]	[illegible]	[illegible]	[illegible]	[illegible]	[illegible]	[illegible]	[illegible]	[illegible]	[illegible]	[illegible]	[illegible]	[illegible]	[illegible]	[illegible]	[illegible]	[illegible]	[illegible]	[illegible]	[illegible]	[illegible]	[illegible]	[illegible]	[illegible]
Texas	[illegible]	[illegible]	[illegible]	[illegible]	[illegible]	[illegible]	[illegible]	[illegible]	[illegible]	[illegible]	[illegible]	[illegible]	[illegible]	[illegible]	[illegible]	[illegible]	[illegible]	[illegible]	[illegible]	[illegible]	[illegible]	[illegible]	[illegible]	[illegible]	[illegible]	[illegible]	[illegible]	[illegible]	[illegible]	[illegible]	[illegible]
Wakeshma	[illegible]	[illegible]	[illegible]	[illegible]	[illegible]	[illegible]	[illegible]	[illegible]	[illegible]	[illegible]	[illegible]	[illegible]	[illegible]	[illegible]	[illegible]	[illegible]	[illegible]	[illegible]	[illegible]	[illegible]	[illegible]	[illegible]	[illegible]	[illegible]	[illegible]	[illegible]	[illegible]	[illegible]	[illegible]	[illegible]	[illegible]

POPULATION BY COUNTIES—1800-1870.

COUNTIES.	AGGREGATE. 1870	1860	1850	1840	1830	1820	1810
Total	1184653	749113	397654	212267	31639	8765	4762
Alcona	696	185					
Allegan	32105	16087	5125	1783			
Alpena	2756	290					
Antrim	1985	179					
Barry	22199	13858	5072	1078			
Bay	15900	3164					
Benzie	2184						
Berrien	35104	22378	11417	5011	325		
Branch	26236	20981	12472	5715			
Brown					1356	952	
Calhoun	36569	29564	19162	10599			
Cass	21094	17721	10907	5710	919		
Charlevoix	1724						
Cheboygan	2196	517					
Chippewa	1689	1603	898	534	626		
Clare	366						
Clinton	22845	13916	1614	1614			
Crawford					692	861	
Delta	2542	1172					
Eaton	25171	16476	7058	2379			
Emmet	1211	1149					
Genesee	33900	22498	12031	4268			
Gladwin		14					
Grand Traverse	4443	1286					
Gratiot	11810	4042					
Hillsdale	31684	25675	16159	7240			
Houghton	13879	9234	708				
Huron	9049	3165	210				
Ingham	25268	17435	8631	2498			
Ionia	27681	16682	7597	1923			
Iosco	3163	175					
Iowa					1587		
Isabella	4113	1443					
Jackson	36047	26671	19431	13130			
Kalamazoo	32054	24646	13179	7380			
Kalkaska	424						
Kent	50403	30716	12016	2587			
Keweenaw	4205						
Lake	548						
Lapeer	21345	14754	7029	4256			
Leelanaw	4576	2158					
Lenawee	45595	38112	26372	17889	1491		
Livingston	19336	16851	13485	7430			
Mackinac	1716						
Macomb	27616	22843	15530	9716	2413	898	580
Manistee	6074	975					
Manitou	891	1042					
Marquette	15033	2821	136				
Mason	3263	831	93				
Mecosta	5342	970					
Menominee	1791						
Michilimackinac		1938	3598	923	877	819	615
Midland	3285	787	65				
Missaukee	130						
Monroe	27483	21593	14698	9922	3187	1831	1340
Montcalm	13629	3968	891				
Montmorency							
Muskegon	14894	3947					
Newaygo	7294	2760	510				
Oakland	40867	38261	31270	23646	4911	330	
Oceana	7222	1816	300	496			
Ogemaw	12						
Ontonagon	2845	4568	389				
Osceola	2093	27					
Oscoda	70						
Otsego							
Ottawa	26651	13215	5587	208			
Presque Isle	355	26					
Roscommon							
Saginaw	39097	12693	2609	892			
Sanilac	14562	7599	2112				
Schoolcraft		78	16				
Shiawassee	20858	12349	5230	2103			
St. Clair	36661	26604	10420	4606	1114		
St. Joseph	26275	21262	12725	7068	1313		
Tuscola	13714	4886	291				
Van Buren	28829	15224	5800	1910	5		
Washtenaw	41434	35686	28567	23571	4042		
Wayne	119038	75547	42756	24173	6781	3574	4237
Wexford	650						

CITIES AND VILLAGES OF MICHIGAN.

CITIES.

Detroit	79,577	Battle Creek	5,838	Manistee	3,343
Grand Rapids	16,507	Ypsilanti	5,471	Grand Haven	3,147
Jackson	11,447	Flint	5,386	Wyandotte	2,731
East Saginaw	11,350	Lansing	5,241	Holland	2,319
Adrian	8,438	Monroe	5,086	Owosso	2,065
Saginaw City	7,460	Marshall	4,925	St. Clair	1,790
Ann Arbor	7,363	Pontiac	4,867	Lapeer	1,772
Bay City	7,064	Niles	4,630	Corunna	1,408
Muskegon	6,002	Coldwater	4,381	Big Rapids	1,237
Port Huron	5,973	Hillsdale	3,518		

VILLAGES.

Kalamazoo	9,181	Plymouth	966	Charleston	471
Marquette	4,000	Schoolcraft	922	Brighton	434
Negaunee	2,559	White Pigeon	922	Copper Falls Mine	434
Ionia	2,306	Morenci	900	Dundee	420
Hudson	2,402	St. Louis	884	Pinckney	450
Allegan	2,374	Ludington	880	Dansville	443
Fenton	2,352	Lexington	840	Davisburgh	440
Charlotte	2,238	Muir	868	Petersburgh	426
Albion	2,100	White Hall	842	New Haven	428
Tecumseh	2,030	Wayne	824	Tawas City	408
Romeo	1,865	Augusta	820	Alma	405
Dowagiac	1,852	Vicksburg	810	Colon	296
St. Johns	1,905	Union City	810	Clio	305
South Saginaw	1,873	Grass Lake	800	Memphis	395
Spring Lake	1,806	Chesaning	787	Ortonville	365
Greenville	1,807	Algonac	751	Waterford	360
Hastings	1,762	Clinton	752	Dansville	315
St. Clair	1,790	Centreville	740	Hilson	351
Mt. Clemens	1,768	Cassopolis	724	Capac	328
Sturgis	1,768	Saranac	724	Vandalia	312
Buchanan	1,792	Burr Oak	724	Orion	304
Wenona	1,651	Ontonagon	721	Fenville	302
Hancock	1,806	Lyons	714	Goodrich	300
South Haven	1,576	Newaygo	700	Edwardsburgh	297
Lockport	1,503	Flushing	687	Dakota	289
Lowell	1,503	Homer	684	Galien	285
Howell	1,469	New Buffalo	681	Otisville	285
Houghton	1,456	Berrien Springs	662	Brooksville	255
Holly	1,429	Mendon	662	St. Joseph	240
Paw Paw	1,428	Oxford	650	Northport	239
Dexter	1,470	Northville	620	Grand Blanc	232
Jonesville	1,361	Bellevue	604	Eagle Harbor	232
Mason	1,314	East Tawas	602	Pokagon	232
Manchester	1,311	Stanton	600	Pine Run	215
Pentwater	1,294	Wayland	586	Watrousville	212
Constantine	1,259	Rockford	582	Flowerfield	210
Portsmouth	1,248	Linden	567	Medina	201
Marine City	1,240	Benton Harbor	561	Port Wayne	188
Eaton Rapids	1,251	Mt. Morris	560	Huntoonville	184
Three Rivers	1,180	Lawrence	555	Cannonsburgh	152
Decatur	1,161	Brooklyn	544	Milan	145
Midland	1,160	Vermontville	511	Morlette	143
Spring Lake	1,136	Nashville	512	Atlas	125
Galesburgh	1,130	Middleville	541	Pierceville	121
Quincy	1,062	Hubbardston	531	Unionville	117
Lawton	1,081	Dearborn	530	Adamsville	104
Portland	1,070	Olivet	522	Gibsonville	100
Ovid	1,090	Three Oaks	492	Richmondville	92
Plainwell	1,055	Armada	484	Hamburgh	81
Saugatuck	1,020	Port Sanilac	481	Case City	59
Chelsea	1,013	Caro	450	Amygdaloid Mine	61
Otsego	1,088	Traverse City	1,080		

TIME AND DISTANCE TABLE.

Showing the Difference in Time and number of Miles between New York and Washington, and the Principal Cities in the Country.

MILES from N. YORK	TIME AT 12 (NOON) IN NEW YORK.	CITIES.	TIME AT 12 (NOON) IN WASHINGTON.	MILES from WASH'N.
150	11 58 A.M.	Albany	12 10 P.M.	371
185	11 50 "	Baltimore	12 02 "	40
236	12 12 P.M.	Boston	12 24 "	461
423	11 40 A.M.	Buffalo	11 52 A.M.	463
898	11 06 "	Chicago	11 18 "	843
799	11 10 "	Cincinnati	11 22 "	601
581	11 30 "	Cleveland	11 42 "	528
650	11 24 "	Columbus	11 36 "	508
703	11 24 "	Detroit	11 32 "	681
825	11 14 "	Indianapolis	11 02 "	776
994	11 14 "	Louisville	11 26 "	781
401	11 38 "	Montreal	12 10 P.M.	662
1557	11 56 "	New Orleans	10 44 A.M.	1022
....	11 12 noon.	New York	12 12 P.M.	224
87	11 40 A.M.	Philadelphia	12 04 "	138
431	11 50 "	Pittsburg	11 48 A.M.	274
358	11 46 "	Richmond	11 58 "	130
1097	11 50 "	St. Louis	11 07 "	874
225	11 48 "	Washington	12 00 noon.	....
550	11 48 "	Wheeling	11 43 A.M.	491

PRINCIPAL GOVERNMENTS OF THE WORLD.

NAME OF COUNTRY.	NAME OF RULER.	TITLE.	FORM OF GOVERNMENT.
Austria	Francis Joseph I.	Emperor	Absolute Monarchy
Argentine Confed'n	D. Mitre	President	Federal Republic
Brazil	Dom Pedro II.	Emperor	Hereditary Monarchy
Chili	Jose Joaq. Perez	President	Republic
China	Kitsiang	Emperor	Absolute Monarchy
Denmark	Christian IX.	King	Lim. Mon. with Two Estates.
Egypt	Ismael Pasha	Viceroy	Absolute Monarchy
France			Const. Mon., Sen. and Legis.
Great Britain	Victoria I.	Queen	Lim. Mon., Lords and Com's.
Greece	George I.	King	Lim. Mon., Two Chambers
Holland	William III.	King	Lim. Mon., Two Chambers
Honduras	Jose Medina	President	Republic
Italy	Victor Emanuel II.	King	Lim. Mon., Two Chambers
Mexico	B. Juarez	President	Republic
Nicaragua	Thomas Martinez	President	Republic
Prussia	William I.	Emperor	Lim. Mon., Two Chambers
Portugal	Luis I.	King	Lim. Mon., One Chamber
Persia	Nasser-e-Din	Schah	Absolute Despotism
Peru	Gen. Prado	President	Republic
Russia	Alexander II.	Czar	Absolute Monarchy
Sweden and Norway	Charles XV.	King	Lim. Mon., with Legislature.
Spain	Amadeus	President	Lim. Mon., with Legislature.
States of the Church	Pius IX.	Pope	Absolute Sovereignty
Switzerland	M. Knusel	Pres. of Diet.	Federative Republic
Turkey	Abdul Aziz	Sultan	Absolute Monarchy
United States	U. S. Grant	President	Fed. Rep., Two Houses Cong.

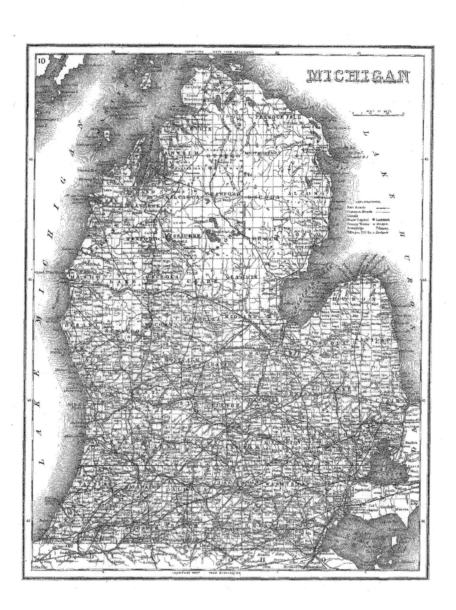

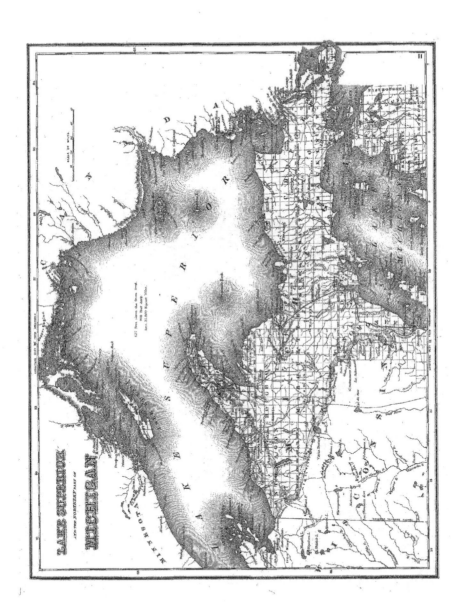

UNITED STATES STATISTICS, Etc., 1870.

PRESENT STATE GOVERNMENTS.				AREA.	POPULATION.		AGRICULTURAL PRODUCTS, ETC.							
STATES.	CAPITALS.	TIME OF STATE ELECTION.	LEGISLATURE MEETS.	AREA IN SQ. MILES.	POP. IN 1870.	POP. IN 1860.	BUSHELS OF WHEAT.	BUSHELS OF CORN.	BUSHELS OF OATS.	TONS OF HAY.	YOUNG CATTLE.	HORSES.	SWINE.	ACRES OF IMP. LAND.
Alabama	Montgomery	Tues. aft. 1 Mon. Nov.	3 Mon. in Nov	50,722	1,002,006	964,201	980,000	30,200,000	367,000	68,000	600,347	150,063	2,500,000	6,385,724
Arkansas	Little Rock	1 Mon. in Nov	1 Mon. in Jan	52,198	478,174	435,450	1,170,000	25,750,000	500,000	10,000	450,005	160,600	1,500,630	1,983,313
California	Sacramento	1 Tues. in Sept.	1 Mon. in Dec	188,981	549,808	379,994	21,500,000	1,305,000	2,000,000	470,000	1,600,000	300,611	2,850,110	2,468,034
Connecticut	Hartford & N. H.	1 Mon. in April	1 Wed. in May	4,751	537,417	460,147	75,000	1,800,000	3,100,000	750,000	112,680	40,150	60,450	1,830,807
Delaware	Dover	1 Tues. in Aug.	1 Tues. in Jan.	2,120	125,015	112,216	830,000	3,200,000	1,722,000	30,000	35,340	21,160	51,200	637,065
Florida	Tallahassee	Tues. aft. 1 Mon. Nov.	Tues. aft. 1 Mon. Jan.	59,248	189,995	140,424	1,200	3,100,000	23,000	13,000	297,680	15,470	299,750	654,213
Georgia	Atlanta	1 Tues. in Aug	2 Wed. in Jan	58,000	1,174,832	1,057,286	2,170,000	27,500,000	1,200,000	48,000	780,350	108,500	2,150,000	8,062,758
Illinois	Springfield	Tues. aft. 1 Mon. Nov.	1 Mon. in Jan	55,201	2,539,410	1,711,951	29,200,000	121,500,000	35,726,000	2,500,000	2,320,500	1,340,290	3,502,820	13,096,374
Indiana	Indianapolis	2 Tues. in Oct	1 Wed. in Jan	33,809	1,655,675	1,350,428	20,600,000	78,000,000	12,418,000	1,300,000	744,850	890,240	3,080,120	8,242,183
Iowa	Des Moines	2 Tues. in Oct	2 Mon. in Jan	55,045	1,181,359	674,913	25,000,000	78,300,000	19,000,000	1,630,000	301,960	190,580	1,001,200	3,792,792
Kansas	Topeka	Tues. aft. 1 Mon. Nov.	2 Tues. in Jan	81,318	379,497	107,206	2,500,000	24,300,000	1,500,000	230,000	71,863	25,301	101,310	405,468
Kentucky	Frankfort	1 Mon. in Aug.	1 Mon. in Dec	37,680	1,320,407	1,155,684	5,000,000	51,300,000	5,800,000	155,000	310,845	650,811	2,090,870	7,644,208
Louisiana	New Orleans	1 Mon. in Nov.	1 Mon. in Jan	41,346	734,420	708,002	50,000	16,850,000	87,000	87,000	320,310	68,320	940,110	2,707,108
Maine	Augusta	2 Mon. in Sept.	1 Wed. in Jan	35,000	628,719	628,279	245,000	1,450,000	2,300,000	1,030,000	230,110	71,110	65,840	2,704,133
Maryland	Annapolis	Tues. aft. 1 Mon. Nov	1 Wed. in Jan	11,124	780,895	687,049	7,758,000	12,300,000	7,100,000	131,000	170,110	99,112	385,120	3,002,267
Massachusetts	Boston	Tues. aft. 1 Mon. Nov.	1 Wed. in Jan	7,800	1,457,351	1,231,066	187,000	1,850,000	1,325,000	690,000	140,340	49,456	98,510	2,155,512
MICHIGAN.	Lansing	Tues. aft. 1 Mon. Nov.	1 Wed. in Jan	**56,451**	**1,184,653**	**749,113**	**16,800,000**	**34,100,000**	**8,700,000**	**1,550,000**	**401,320**	**301,340**	**640,960**	**3,475,295**
Minnesota	St. Paul	Tues. aft. 1 Mon. Nov.	Tues. aft. 1 Mon. Jan.	83,531	434,548	172,023	10,000,000	3,750,000	12,500,000	598,000	38,470	45,780	150,580	556,250
Mississippi	Jackson	Tues. aft. 1 Mon. Nov.	Tues. aft. 1 Mon. Jan.	47,156	842,056	791,305	287,000	30,000,000	230,000	40,000	600,708	117,870	1,780,101	5,065,755
Missouri	Jefferson City	Tues. aft. 1 Mon. Nov.	Last Mon. in Dec	65,350	1,681,093	1,182,012	7,500,000	80,300,000	6,500,000	750,000	700,112	520,640	2,700,800	6,246,871
Nebraska	Lincoln	2 Tues. in Oct.	Thurs. aft. 1 Mon. Jan.	75,995	116,888	28,841	1,000,000	6,750,000	1,250,000	110,000	......	......	......	......
Nevada	Carson City	Tues. aft. 1 Mon. Nov.	1 Mon. in Jan	81,539	42,439	Nev. & Ter.	2,500,000	2,000,000	1,500,000	......	......	......	......	......
New Hampshire	Concord	2 Tues. in March	1 Mon. in June	9,280	317,710	326,073	221,000	1,400,000	1,938,000	700,000	263,890	45,101	79,690	2,367,034
New Jersey	Trenton	Tues. aft. 1 Mon. Nov.	2 Tues. in Jan	8,320	903,044	672,035	1,686,000	9,200,000	6,140,000	525,000	98,450	85,480	300,340	1,944,441
New York	Albany	Tues. aft. 1 Mon. Nov.	1 Tues. in Jan	47,000	4,370,846	3,880,735	9,750,000	19,100,000	31,250,000	4,500,000	2,450,800	703,120	4,060,300	14,358,403
North Carolina	Raleigh	1 Thurs. in Aug	1 Thurs. in Nov	50,704	1,016,954	992,622	3,870,000	17,400,000	3,300,000	160,000	591,190	160,308	1,808,200	6,517,284
Ohio	Columbus	2 Tues. in Oct	1 Mon. in Jan	39,964	2,652,302	2,339,511	20,400,000	68,250,000	27,000,000	3,000,000	1,060,350	1,200,000	3,880,000	12,625,394
Oregon	Salem	1 Mon. in June	2 Mon. in Sept	95,274	90,878	52,465	1,750,000	200,000	500,000	75,000	140,500	49,800	112,700	896,414
Pennsylvania	Harrisburg	2 Tues. in Oct	1 Tues. in Jan	46,000	3,511,543	2,906,215	16,800,000	23,500,000	48,000,000	2,570,000	880,400	962,300	1,748,040	10,463,296
Rhode Island	Prov. & N'port.	1 Wed. in April	May and Jan	1,306	217,356	174,620	8,500	440,000	250,000	71,000	21,420	9,140	21,060	335,128
South Carolina	Columbia	4 Mon. in Nov	2 Wed. in Oct	34,000	705,789	703,708	920,000	8,100,000	850,000	58,000	249,890	96,125	1,090,720	4,572,060
Tennessee	Nashville	1 Mon. in Aug.	1 Mon. in Oct	45,600	1,225,937	1,109,801	6,750,000	47,500,000	3,500,000	168,000	709,330	300,275	2,800,312	6,795,337
Texas	Austin	1 Mon. in Aug.	1 Mon. in Nov	274,356	800,000	604,215	1,250,000	21,000,000	1,250,000	28,000	2,540,300	600,250	1,580,800	2,650,781
Vermont	Montpelier	1 Tues. in Sept	2 Thurs. in Oct	10,212	330,582	315,098	705,000	1,475,000	5,050,000	1,100,000	230,300	71,840	81,450	2,823,157
Virginia	Richmond	Tues. aft. 1 Mon. Nov.	1 Mon. in Dec	38,352	1,211,442	1,596,318	8,642,000	17,500,000	9,017,000	220,000	917,250	420,960	1,900,300	11,437,821
West Virginia	Charleston	4 Thurs. in Oct	2 Tues. in Jan	23,000	441,094		2,562,000	8,100,000	2,100,000	150,000				
Wisconsin	Madison	Tues. aft. 1 Mon. Nov.	1 Wed. in Jan	53,924	1,055,501	775,881	24,000,000	9,800,000	22,000,000	1,250,000	480,819	140,969	865,908	3,746,167
						Total	264,146,900	874,120,005	268,284,000	26,420,000	21,314,008	10,081,676	46,045,607	162,753,798

TERRITORIES.	CAPITALS.	SQ. MILES.	POP. IN 1870.	TERRITORIES.	CAPITALS.	SQ. MILES.	POP. IN 1870.	TERRITORIES.	CAPITALS.	SQ. MILES.	POP. IN 1870.	TOTAL STATISTICS OF UNITED STATES.	
Alaska	Sitka	394,000	67,000	Idaho	Boise	91,000	14,882	Utah	Salt Lake City	88,000	70,000	Sq. miles	3,400,000
Arizona	Tucson	114,000	9,658	Indian	Tahlequah	69,000	37,812	Washington	Olympia	70,000	20,925	Pop. in 1870	38,312,629
Colorado	Denver	103,000	39,681	Montana	Virginia City	144,000	20,594	Wyoming	Cheyenne	102,000	9,118	Pop. in 1860	31,443,321
Dakota	Yankton	148,000	14,181	New Mexico	Santa Fe	122,000	93,516	Dist. of Columbia	Washington	60	131,706		

CENSUS OF KALAMAZOO COUNTY,

BY TOWNSHIPS.

Year of Organization.	COUNTIES, CITIES AND TOWNSHIPS.	Total Population.	Number of Families.	Number of Dwellings.	Sex Stated.	Total Number of each Sex.
1830	**KALAMAZOO CO.**	32065	6824	6347	M F	16522 15543
1838	Alamo	1149	241	235	M F	601 548
1842	Brady	1382	290	286	M F	717 665
1838	Charleston	1369	281	277	M F	737 632
1838	Climax	1389	269	270	M F	740 649
1839	Comstock	2023	391	397	....	1033 990
1839	Cooper	1254	277	270	....	667 587
1830	Kalamazoo	10450	1890	1901	M F	5177 5273
1839	Oshtemo	1594	322	326	M F	832 762
1836	Pavilion	1208	248	249	....	643 565
1838	Portage	1050	211	208	....	563 487
1830	Prairie Ronde	1164	223	209	....	641 523
1832	Richland	1380	270	271	....	730 650
1839	Ross	2005	413	421	...	1005 1000
1830	Schoolcraft	2137	463	443	M F	1095 1042
1838	Texas	1110	230	225	M F	582 528
1846	Wakeshma	1401	290	299	M F	753 648

POST OFFICES KALAMAZOO CO., Mich.

	In what Township located.
Alamo	Alamo
Augusta	Ross
Brady	Brady
Climax	Climax
Comstock	Comstock
Cooper	Cooper
Fulton	Wakeshma
Galesburgh, Money Order Office	Comstock
Kalamazoo, County Seat & Money Order Office	Kalamazoo
Oshtemo	Oshtemo
Pavilion	Pavilion
Portage	Portage
Richland	Richland
Schoolcraft	Schoolcraft
South Climax	Climax
Wakeshma	Wakeshma
Yorkville	Ross
Vicksburg	Schoolcraft
Scotts	Pavilion

THE UNITED STATES,

WHEN, WHERE, AND BY WHOM SETTLED.

YEAR OF SETTLEMENT.	STATES.	AREA IN SQUARE MILES.	WHERE SETTLED.	BY WHOM.
1565	Florida	59,268	St. Augustine	Spaniards.
1607	Virginia	61,352	Jamestown	English.
1614	New York	47,000	Manhattan	Dutch.
1620	Massachusetts	7,800	Plymouth	English Puritans.
1623	New Hampshire	9,280	Dover	English.
1624	New Jersey	8,320	Bergen	Dutch and Danes.
1630	Maine	31,766	Bristol	English.
1627	Delaware	2,120	Cape Henlopen	Swedes and Finns.
1635	Connecticut	4,674	Windsor	Emigration from Mass.
1634	Maryland	11,124	St. Mary's	English.
1636	Rhode Island	1,306	Providence	English.
1663	North Carolina	50,704	Albemarle	English.
1669	Wisconsin	53,924	Green Bay	French.
1670	Michigan	56,243	Detroit	French.
1670	South Carolina	29,385	Port Royal	English.
1682	Pennsylvania	46,000	Philadelphia	English.
1685	Arkansas	52,198	Arkansas Post	French.
1690	Texas	237,504	San Antonio de Bexar	Spaniards.
1690	Indiana	33,809	Vincennes	French.
1699	Louisiana	41,346	Iberville	French.
1711	Alabama	50,722	Mobile	French.
1716	Mississippi	47,156	Natchez	French.
1720	Illinois	55,405	Kaskaskia	French.
1725	Vermont	10,212	Fort Dummer	Emigration from Mass.
1733	Georgia	58,000	Savannah	English.
1757	Tennessee	45,600	Fort London	Emigration from N. C.
1764	Missouri	67,380	St. Louis	French.
1769	California	188,981	San Diego	Spaniards.
1775	Kentucky	37,680	Boonesboro	Emigration from Va.
1788	Ohio	39,964	Marietta	Emi. from N. England.
1811	Oregon	102,606	Astoria	Emi. from N. York.
1833	Iowa	55,045	Burlington	Emi. from N. England.
1846	Minnesota	83,531	St. Paul	Emi. from N. England.
1850	Kansas	78,418	Fort Leavenworth	Emi. fr. N. E. & W. Sts.
1850	Nevada	81,539	Washoe City	Emi. fr. Cal. principally.
....	West Virginia	24,000	......	Formed fr. State of Va.

PLAN OF

KALAMAZOO CO.

MICHIGAN

Scale 24 Miles to the inch

ALLEGAN COUNTY

BARRY COUNTY

RANGE XII WEST   RANGE XI WEST   RANGE X WEST   RANGE IX WEST

ALAMO   COOPER   RICHLAND   ROSS

VAN   BUREN   COUNTY

Township II South

Township III South

Township IV South

OSHTEMO   KALAMAZOO   COMSTOCK   CHARLESTON

TEXAS   PORTAGE   PAVILION   CLIMAX

PRAIRIE   SCHOOLCRAFT   BRADY   WAKESHMA

RONDE

RANGE XII WEST   RANGE XI WEST   RANGE X WEST   RANGE IX WEST

St. JOSEPH COUNTY

CALHOUN COUNTY

ALAMO

Township 1 South   Range XII West.

Scale 1¾ inches to the mile.

A L L E G A N   CO.

ALLEGAN COUNTY

H.G.Wells 133 a.   145 a.   136 a.   J. Rose

DIST. No 2

D. Howard   E. Merry   W. Stevens

E. Hurt   J. Hopkins

P. Holmes 120 a.   H. Hall

R. Fisher

J. Brown 60 a.   J.Murray 160 a.   N.R.Rose 120 a.

DIST. No 3

C.& J. Ransom 604 a.

G.W. Bliss 120 a.   G.W. Bliss 100 a.   B. Rose

E.P. Hackley   J. Hackley 240 a.   Geo. Piper   DIST. No

E. Tallman 160 a.

Miss J. Pratt 160 a.

FRAC DIST No

ALAMO CENTRE P.O.

H.A. Tallman   A. Tallman 160 a.

J.M. Veley   E. Davis

S.H. Simmons 160 a.

Green Freeman

DIST No

W. Payson 160 a.

FRAC DIST No 5

C.K. Clark 100 a.   H. Fox

E. Bigelow 150 a.   DIST No 3

H. McCall   FRAC DIST No 4   B. Snow 80 a.

W. Pyburn 180 a.   E. Wolcott

De Wolters 160 a.   Cne Reynolds 100 a.   S. Batch

O S H T E M O

ALLEGAN CO.

ALAMO CENTRE
ALAMO TP.
Scale 20 Rods to the inch

COOPER CENTER
COOPER TP.
Scale 20 Rods to the inch

Alamo Township.
Business Notices

Cooper Township
Business Notices

Cooper Center
Business Notices

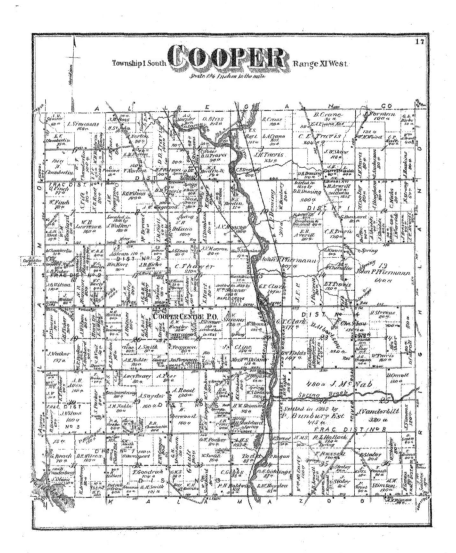

COOPER

Township I South   Range XI West.

Scale 1¼ Inches to the mile.

RICHLAND

Township 1 South   Range X West.

Scale 1¾ inches to the mile.

BARRY CO.

Gull Lake

Richland P.O.

DIST. No 8   DIST. No 19   DIST. No 1

DIST. No 2   DIST. No 5   DIST. No 6

DIST. No 3   DIST. No 10   DIST. No 9

DIST. No 4

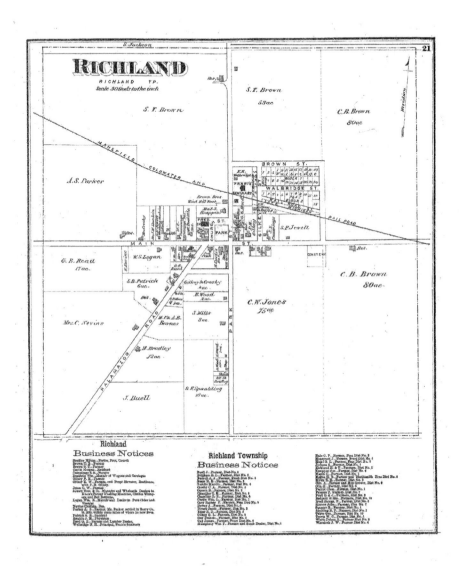

RICHLAND

RICHLAND TP.
Scale 30 rods to the inch

Richland
Business Notices

Bradley Milton - Pastor, Pres. Church
Brown G. B. - Farmer
Brown S. T. - Farmer
Curtis Morgan - Resident
Cummings S. S. - Farmer
Doolittle Wm. - Manuf'r of Wagons and Carriages
Gilkey B. K. - Farmer
Gilkey E. W. - Farmer, and Prop'r Elevator, Residence, with P. H. Gilkey.
Jones C. W. - Farmer
Jewett Bros. & Co. - Manufrs and Wholesale Dealers in Kban's Patent Washing Machines, Clothes Wringers, and Bed Bottoms.
Logan Wm. S. - Farmer and Dealer in Pure Cider and Vinegar
Nevins Cynthia, Mrs.
Parker A. S. - Farmer, Mr. Parker settled in Barry Co. in 1839, within three miles of where he now lives.
Patrick S. B. - Resident
Smith S. M. - Physician
Reed G. E. - Farmer and Lumber Dealer
Walbridge H. S. - Principal, Prairie Seminary

Richland Township
Business Notices

Buell J. - Farmer, Dist No. 3
Brigham R. L. - Farmer, Dist No. 1
Burrell A. J. - Farmer, Front Dist No. 1
Buell M. B. - Farmer, Dist No. 1
Burdic March. - Farmer, Dist No. 1
Crosby G. A. - Farmer, Dist No. 2
Garwin M. - Farmer, Dist No. 2
Chandler G. H. - Farmer, Dist No. 2
Chandler D. S. - Farmer, Dist No. 3
Curtis Wm. R. - Farmer, Dist No. 3
Cory Barney W. - Farmer, Frac Dist No. 2
Darboy J. J. - Farmer, Dist No. 2
Drury Jacob - Farmer, Dist No. 3
Riter S. J. - Farmer, Dist No. 3
Gilkey G. L. - Farmer, Dist No. 1
Gay Francis - Farmer, Dist No. 1
Gay James - Farmer, Front Dist No. 1
Humphrey Wm. E. - Farmer and Stock Dealer, Dist No. 1

Hale G. P. - Farmer, Frac Dist No. 2
Honeywell J. - Farmer, Front Dist No. 1
Higgs G. L. - Farmer, Frac Dist No. 1
Johnson L. - Farmer, Dist No. 1
Kinball H. T. - Farmer, Dist No. 3
Longyor Geo. - Farmer, Dist No. 2
Merrill S. - Farmer, Dist No. 1
Maiden H. D. - Farmer and Blacksmith, Frac Dist No. 2
Miller S. N. - Farmer, Dist No. 2
Otis R. - Farmer and Hop Grower, Dist No. 2
Otis E. - Farmer, Dist No. 2
Parker Chas. - Farmer, Dist No. 1
Prosser E. - Farmer, Dist No. 2
Pratt O. J. - Farmer, Dist No. 3
Redfield A. Geo. - Farmer, Dist No. 10
Reed George F. - Farmer, Dist No. 2
Simons Adam - Farmer, Dist No. 2
Spooner S. - Farmer, Dist No. 1
Spalding R. F. - Farmer, Dist No. 2
Taylor Geo. - Farmer, Dist No. 10
Travis D. S. - Farmer, Dist No. 1
White John - Farmer, Dist No. 1
Wright D. - Farmer, Dist No. 1

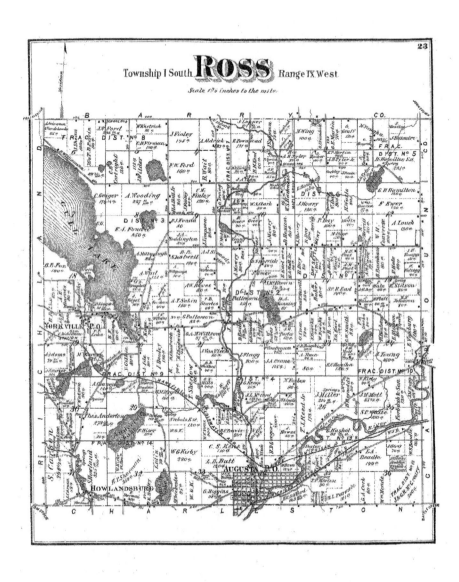

Township I South **Ross** Range IX West

Scale 1¼ inches to the mile.

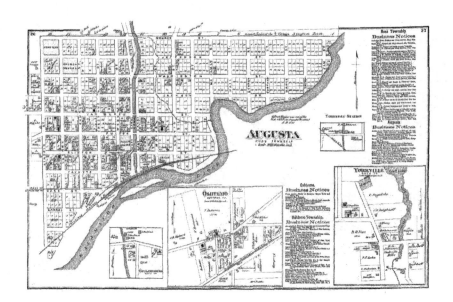

OSHTEMO

Township II South **OSHTEMO** Range XII West

Scale 1¼ Inches to the mile

KALAMAZOO

Township II South Range XI West

Scale 1¾ Inches to the mile

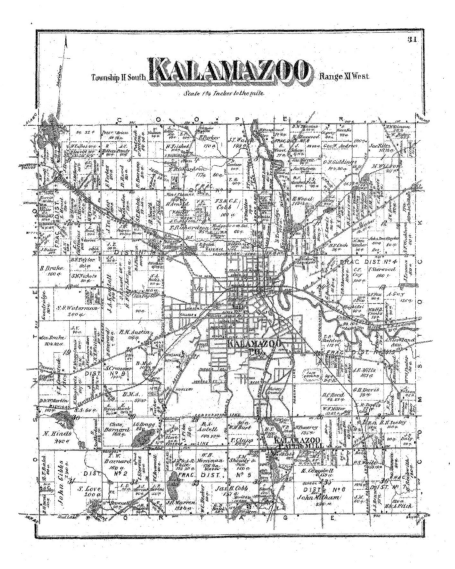

Kalamazoo Township Business Notices.

KALAMAZOO BUSINESS NOTICES.

County Officers

Village Officers

Attorneys

Agents

Agricultural Implements

Banks

Boots and Shoes

Builders

Books and Stationery

Clothiers and Gents' Furnishers

City Bakery

Druggists

Dry Goods

Dentists

Furniture

Kalamazoo Business Notices Continued on Page 34.

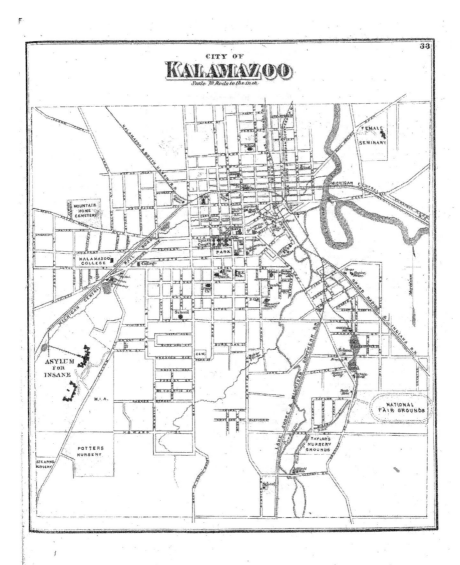

CITY OF
KALAMAZOO
Scale 70 Rods to the inch.

Kalamazoo Business Notices,

Continued from Page 32.

Groceries and Provisions

Hotels

Hardware

Harness

Jewelers

Liveries

Lumber Dealers

Merchant Millers

Fish

Merchants

Music and Musical Instruments

Manufacturers

Markets

Masons

Nurserymen

Officers

Publishers and Printers

Physicians

Photographers

Produce Merchants

Plumbers and Gas Fitters

Painters

Restaurants

Sewing Machines

Schools

Saloons

Tobacco and Cigars

Miscellaneous

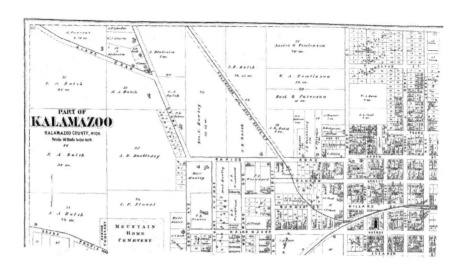

PART OF
KALAMAZOO
KALAMAZOO COUNTY, MICH.
Scale 16 Rods to the inch.

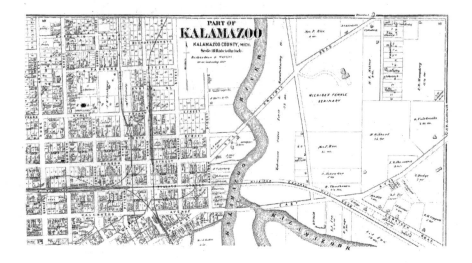

PART OF
KALAMAZOO
KALAMAZOO COUNTY, MICH.
Scale 18 Rods to the inch.

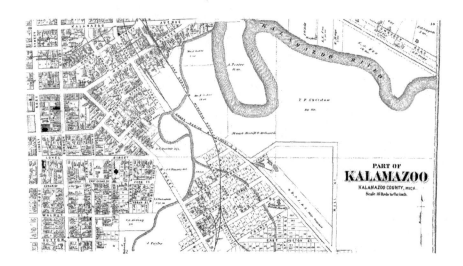

PART OF
KALAMAZOO
KALAMAZOO COUNTY, MICH.
Scale 16 Rods to the Inch.

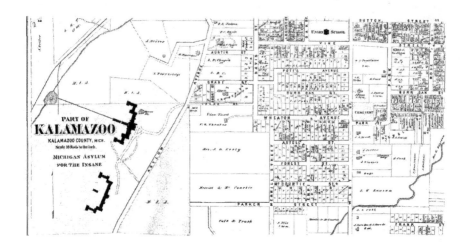

PART OF
KALAMAZOO
KALAMAZOO COUNTY, MICH.
Scale 16 Rods to the inch

NATIONAL FAIR GROUNDS

PART OF
KALAMAZOO

KALAMAZOO COUNTY, MICH.
Scale 16 Rods to the inch.

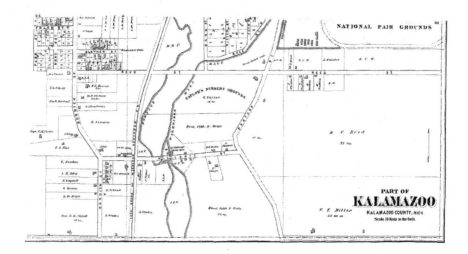

PART OF
KALAMAZOO
KALAMAZOO COUNTY, MICH.
Scale 10 Rods to the Inch.

COMSTOCK

Township II South **COMSTOCK** Range X West

Scale 1¾ Inches to the mile

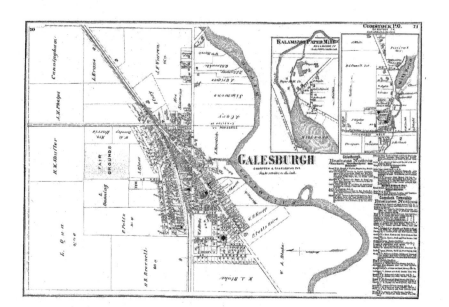

CHARLESTON

Township II South Range IX West

Scale 1¼ inches to the mile

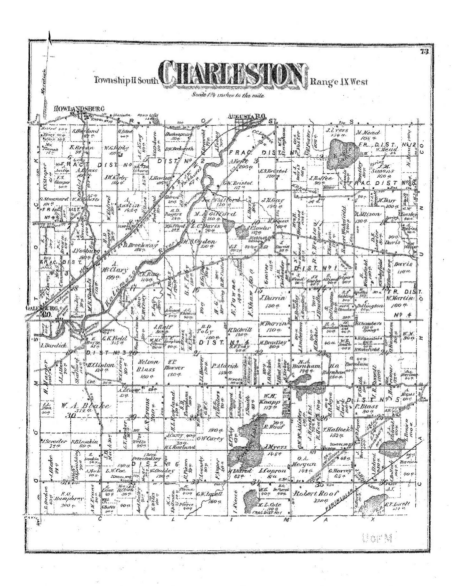

Township III South **TEXAS** Range XII West

Scale 1¼ Inches to the mile

O S H T E M O

R.Allen
J.Rix
I.Rix 155 a.
J.Morgan
E.H.Davis

D.K.Rix 154 a.
N.C.Lapham
DIST. Nº 4
J.W.Fellows
R.Putney
FRAC. DIST. Nº 2

FRAC. DIST. Nº 6
J.Dykeman
J.H.Bucknell
W.H.Howe
J.Clifford 300 a.

G.B.Rix
C.L.Rix
F.D.Rix
A.Vanam
E.Haines
F.Ott
L.R.Clapp
E.Val

N.Easton
J.D.Rix 155 a.
N.Atwater
C.McLean
A.Fee
Campbell Brothers 207 a.

E.Easton
C.Hontey
P.Stafford
W.Adams
W.A.Borden
DIST. Nº 4
H.B.Douglass

Holdings 100 a.
A.White
J.&G.Gildken
A.J.Steele 104 a.
J.Angell
R.A.Towers
N.Burney
C.W.Whipple

J.Jones
J.A.Steele
E.Clapp
BROOKS
Harrison
A.Bell
Jas. McElroy

DIST. Nº 10
N.K.Hunt 150 a.
O.B.Bryan
D.Benling
S.Morgan 100 a.
T.Stanley 100 a.

Non Resident
Hunt & Buck 50 a.
J.J.Shaw Jr.
A.B.Stewart
C.Weed 100 a.
D.G.North
E.Douglass
E.N.Elroy

S.G.Williams 80 a.
A.B.Hill
E.Weed 145 a.
L.Edmunds 65 a.

S.Ferro 130 a.
W.E.Stewart
L.S.Bardick
E.Hope 160 a.
L.A.Parsons
S.Powers 150 a.

FRAC DIST Nº 7
H.Hixson 190 a.
L.Shardick 140 a.
N.Lare
Kinney
FRAC. DIST. Nº 1
J.Wells 155 a.

J.Orland
B.Harrison
F.Clark 180 a.
Aldrich
F.St.J. Harrison 160 a.
E.J. Fellows 120 a.
Lydia J. Bassett 240 a.
N.Knapp

DIST Nº 11

P R A I R I E   R O N D E

PORTAGE

Township III South Range XI West

Scale 1¾ Inches to the mile

(Map of Portage Township, Kalamazoo County, showing landowner parcels, roads, lakes including West Lake and Austin Lake, Austin Station, Portage Center P.O., and fractional school districts.)

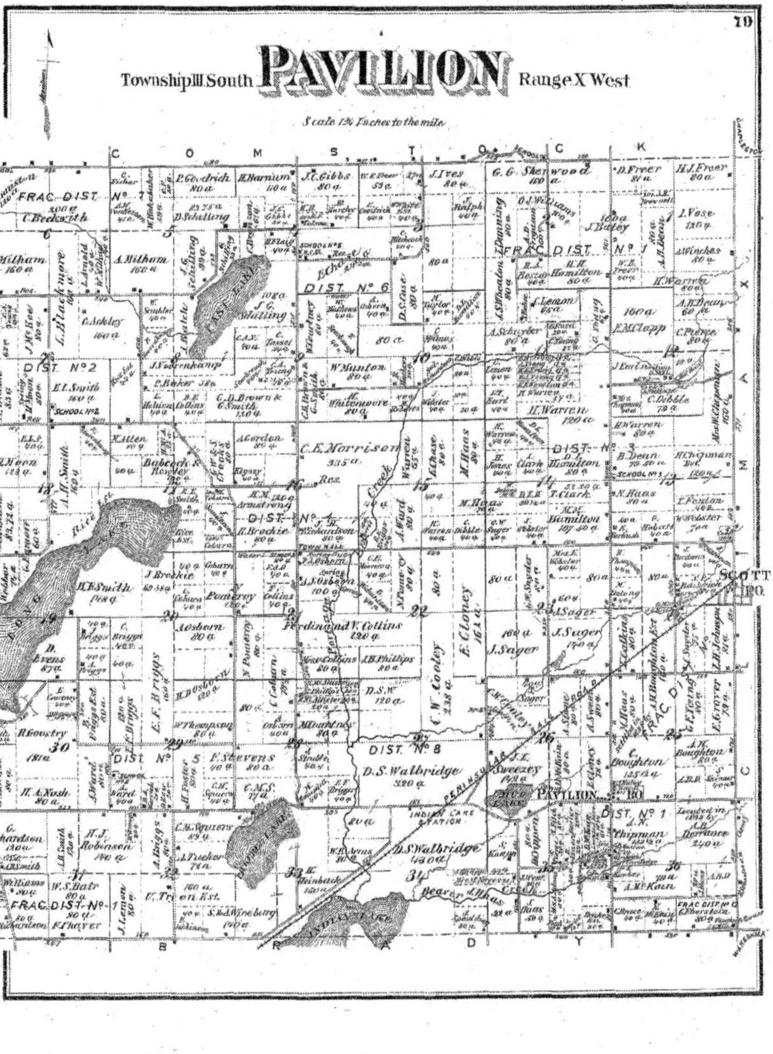
Township III South
PAVILION
Range X West
Scale 1¾ Inches to the mile
C O M S T O C K
P O R T A G E
T E X A S
B R A D Y
FRAC DIST No 7
DIST No 2
DIST No 6
FRAC DIST No 1
DIST No 3
DIST No 4
DIST No 5
DIST No 8
DIST No 1
FRAC DIST No 1
C.E.Morrison 335 a
D.S.Walbridge 320 a
D.S.Walbridge 480 a
C.W.Cooley 238 a
E.F.Briggs
A.Milham 160 a
J.G.Schilling
G.G.Sherwood 160 a
H.Warren 120 a
E.C.Cooley 161 a
J.Sager
Ferdinand V. Collins 120 a
SCOTT P.O.
PAVILION P.O.
PENINSULAR RAIL ROAD
INDIAN LAKE STATION
Echo Lake
Long Lake
Indian Lake
Eagle Lake
Creek
SCHOOL No 2
SCHOOL No 6
SCHOOL No 3

CLIMAX

Township III South   Range IX West

Scale 1½ Inches to the mile.

CHARLESTON

DIST. No 3

CLIMAX P.O.

FRAC. DIST. No

DIST. No 5

DIST. No 2

DIST. No 8

DIST. No 4

SOUTH CLIMAX P.O.

DIST. No 6

DIST. No 7

SCOTTS P.O.

FRAC. DIST No 9

PREMIUM FARM OF MICHIGAN
J.D.Adams
500 a.

E.O.Humphrey 215 a.

J.Bailey

W.R.Bellows 320 a.

I.Pierce 85 a.

G.W. Lowell 165 a.

I.Pierce 235 a.

J.Sherman

J.Schramlin 167 a.

E.T.Lovell 171 a.

A.N.LeFevre

H.H. Pierce 160 a.

N.Eldred

Sheldon

C.W. Eldred

Weldick

R.N.Davis 160 a.

H.Cook

C.B. Guchess 160 a.

A.N. LeFevre 159 a.

Wm.Richards

T.B. Eldred 158 a.

S.Eldred

I.Schramlin

J.F.Weldick

Q.E.Davis

S.T. Averill 164 a.

S.Milliman 160 a.

P.C.Pearce 200 a.

S.Carney 140 a.

H.R.Howard

I.Pierce 160 a.

N.Eldred

H.Cole

A.Woodin 640 a.

E.D.Todd

T.Hayden

R.Childs

D.C.Powers 200 a.

G.Sheldon 90 a.

Knapp & Smith 160 a.

J.B.Eldred 160 a.

B.Persell

T.Pease

J.Roe

L.Stewart

W.Platt

T.B.Eldred 160 a.

F.Phelps

H.Day

J.Van

J.Sayer

D.K.Snyder

H.Myers

L.W.Johnson

S.Sayer

J.Harrison

J.B.Reynolds

E.Grover

L.R.Cooley

H.Byron

B.Harrison

J.Sayer

S.Bayer

H.Roe

D.Clement 100 a.

H.Root

S.Lawrence

W.Preston
C.Wedell

I.Langman

N.Tupper

V.Chapin

E.Hazlett

J.Kellet
S.Adams

J.Selborn

L.S.

Eastman

WAKESHMA

BRADY

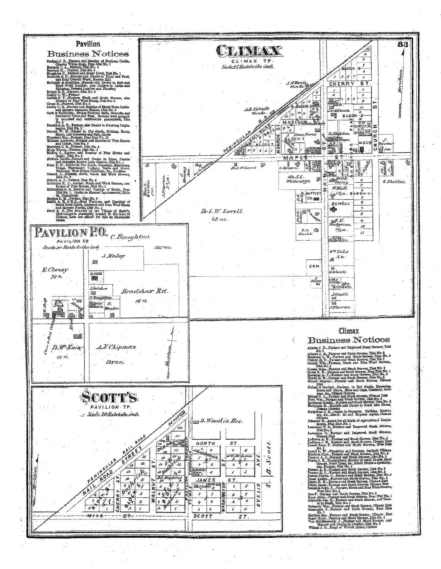

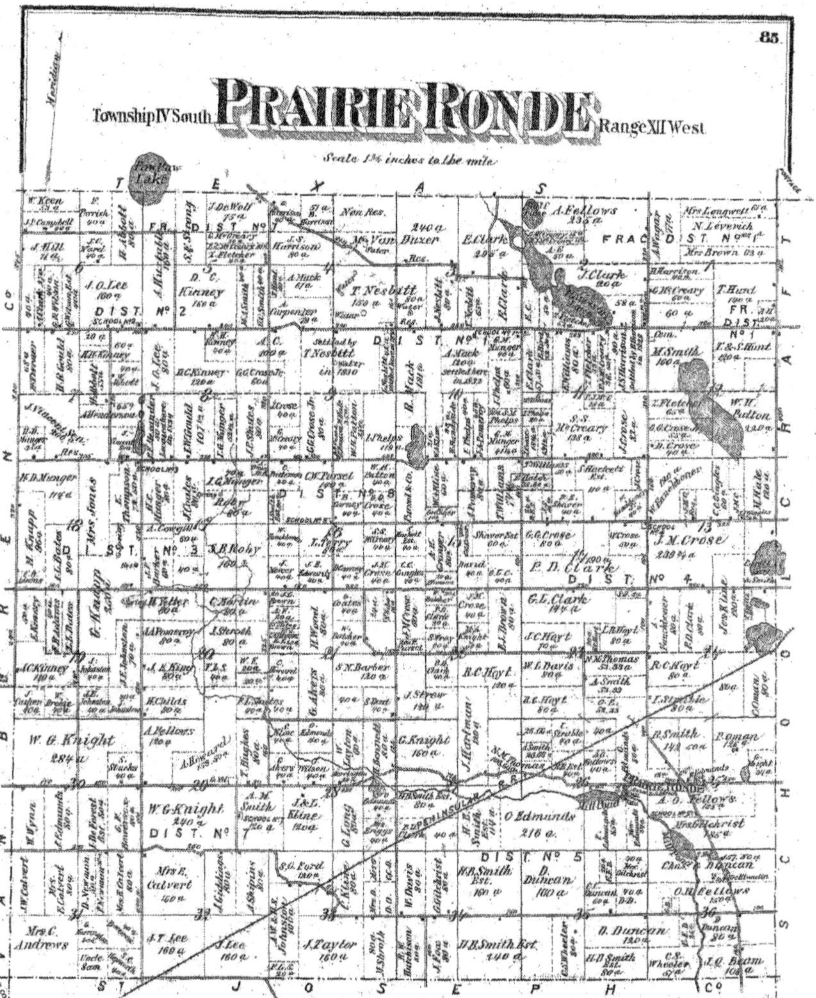

Township IV South
PRAIRIE RONDE
Range XII West
Scale 1¾ inches to the mile
Meridian
Paw Paw Lake
T E X A S
S T J O S E P H C°
V A N B U R E N C°
S C H O O L C R A F T
W. G. Knight 284 a
W. G. Knight 240 a
T. Nesbitt 150 a
Settled by T. Nesbitt in 1830
J. O. Lee 160 a
D. C. Kinney 160 a
A. Fellows 235 a
J. Clark 80 a
N. Leverich
Mrs Brown 63 a
E. Clark 295 a
M. Smith 160 a
W. H. Bulton 230 a
J. M. Crose 232 ½ a
P. D. Clark 190 a
G. L. Clark 147 a
J. C. Hoyt 70 a
R. C. Hoyt
W. L. Davis 90 a
O. Edmunds 216 a
D. Duncan 160 a
D. Duncan 120 a
O. H. Fellows 150 a
A. O. Fellows 125 a
Mrs Gilchrist 195 a
J. Q. Beam 105 a
H. B. Smith Est. 140 a
H. B. Smith Est. 160 a
J. Taylor 160 a
J. Lee 160 a
J. T. Lee 160 a
Mrs C. Andrews
Mrs E. Calvert 160 a
W. Calvert
G. Knight 160 a
J. Strow 120 a
S. N. Barber 120 a
S. B. Roby 160 a
C. W. Porset 160 a
G. Kadley 250 a
Mrs Jones
H. D. Munger 116 a
A. C. Kinney 110 a
DIST. N° 1
DIST. N° 2
DIST. N° 3
DIST. N° 4
DIST. N° 5
DIST. N° 8
FRAC DIST. N° 1
FR. DIST. N° 1
PENINSULAR R. R.
Prairie Ronde
Non Res.
240 a
Van Duzer

SCHOOLCRAFT

Township IV South Range XI West

Scale 1¼ Inches to the mile

SCHOOLCRAFT

SCHOOLCRAFT TP.

Scale 400 Feet to the inch.

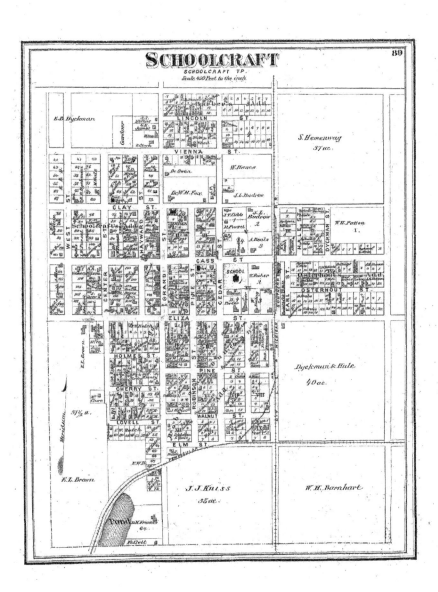

E.B. Dykeman.

Gardner.

S. Hemenway
37 ac.

LINCOLN ST.

VIENNA ST.

Dr. Owen.

W.Hanes

Dr.W.H.Fox

J.L.Badrow

CLAY ST.

J.T.Cobb

J.L.Badrow
2

R.Powel

WEST ST.

Schoolcraft

A.Beals
3

W.H.Patton
1.

HALL ST.

DYCKMAN ST.

CASS ST.

SCHOOL

W.Fisher

CENTER ST.

GRAND ST.

PINE ST.

CEDAR ST.

Dr.A.Fisher

OSTERHOUT ST.

EARL ST.

ELIZA ST.

HOLMES ST.

Dyekman & Hale
40 ac.

E.L.Brown.

CHERRY ST.

PINE ST.

ROBINSON ST.

WALNUT ST.

37½ a.

COVELL ST.

Meridian

ELM ST.

E.W.H.

F.L. Brown.

J.J.Kniss
35 ac.

W.H. Barnhart

Vroom N.K.Brown's
6 a.

F.Dell.

Kalamazoo County Business Notices.

Schoolcraft

Bank

Editor and Printer.

Hotel

Manufacturers

Merchants

Miscellaneous

Physicians

Schoolcraft Township

Vicksburg

Hotel

Merchants

Brady

Charleston.

Texas Township

Portage

Prairie Ronde Township

Wakeshma

Wakeshma Centre

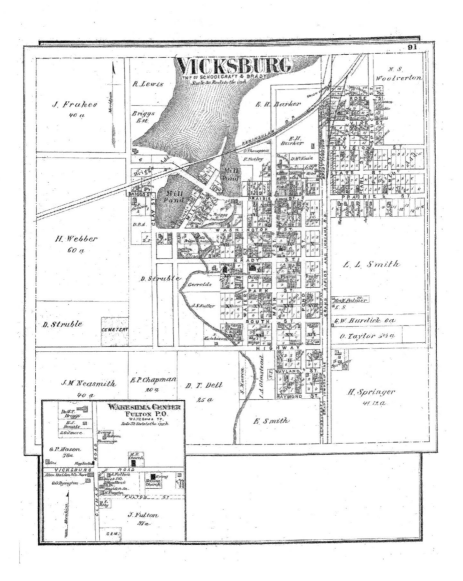

VICKSBURG
TN F OF SCHOOLCRAFT & BRADY
Scale 20 Rods to the inch

J. Frakes
40 a

R. Lewis

Briggs
Est.

E. H. Barker

N. S.
Woolverton

H. Webber
60 a

D. Struble

D. Struble

CEMETERY

L. L. Smith

G. W. Burdick 6 a

O. Taylor 5⅓ a

J. M. Neasmith
40 a

E. P. Chapman
20 a

D. T. Dell
25 a

F. Smith

H. Springer
41.12 a

WAKESHMA CENTER
FULTON P.O.
WAKESHMA TP.
Scale 33 Rods to the inch

G. P. Mason
76 a

VICKSBURG

J. Fulton
87 a

CEM.

Township IV South **BRADY** Range X West

Scale 134 Inches to the mile

Indian Lake

VICKSBURG

A.D. Riley

Jac. Lemon

B.S. Williams

Worthington

A.S. Brockway

J.Wilson

J.Lemmon

G.W.Brockway

W.Best

J.M.Blair

W.Jenkinson

H.Best

W. Southworth

S.Collins

D.E. Rishel

P. Stroine

J.Rishel

E.B. Wandell

E.Kimble

W.Kimble

L.Rapp

L.Brunson

W.R.Dickerson

A.Best

J.Webster

C.Brown

R.Axtell

W.Axtell

J.Brown

H.Robinson

W.Dent

J.Darling

F.Kuhn

C.Lowe

S.Hoch

N.Specht

D.W.Payn

Osgood

WAKESHMA

Township IV South   Range IX West

Scale 1¼ Inches to the mile